YOUR KNOWLEDGE HAS VALUE

- We will publish your bachelor's and master's thesis, essays and papers

- Your own eBook and book - sold worldwide in all relevant shops

- Earn money with each sale

Upload your text at www.GRIN.com and publish for free

Charles Mensah

A Review of the National Health Insurance Scheme and the Possibility of a Single Premium for a Decade

GRIN Verlag

Bibliografische Information der Deutschen Nationalbibliothek:

Die Deutsche Bibliothek verzeichnet diese Publikation in der Deutschen National-
bibliografie; detaillierte bibliografische Daten sind im Internet über http://dnb.d-
nb.de/ abrufbar.

Imprint:

Copyright © 2010 GRIN Verlag GmbH
Druck und Bindung: Books on Demand GmbH, Norderstedt Germany
ISBN: 978-3-656-43333-0

This book at GRIN:

http://www.grin.com/en/e-book/214793/a-review-of-the-national-health-insurance-
scheme-and-the-possibility-of

Dieses Werk sowie alle darin enthaltenen einzelnen Beiträge und Abbildungen sind urheberrechtlich geschützt. Jede Verwertung, die nicht ausdrücklich vom Urheberrechtsschutz zugelassen ist, bedarf der vorherigen Zustimmung des Verlages. Das gilt insbesondere für Vervielfältigungen, Bearbeitungen, Übersetzungen, Mikroverfilmungen, Auswertungen durch Datenbanken und für die Einspeicherung und Verarbeitung in elektronische Systeme.

Inhalt

This book is also...

GRIN - Your knowledge has value

Der GRIN Verlag publiziert seit 1998 wissenschaftliche Arbeiten von Studenten, Hochschullehrern und anderen Akademikern als eBook und gedrucktes Buch. Die Verlagswebsite www.grin.com ist die ideale Plattform zur Veröffentlichung von Hausarbeiten, Abschlussarbeiten, wissenschaftlichen Aufsätzen, Dissertationen und Fachbüchern.

Visit us on the internet:

http://www.grin.com/

http://www.facebook.com/grincom

http://www.twitter.com/grin_com

UNIVERSITY FOR DEVELOPMENT STUDIES

(UDS)

A REVIEW OF THE NATIONAL HEALTH INSURANCE SCHEME AND THE POSSIBILITY OF A SINGLE PREMIUM FOR A DECADE

"A CASE STUDY OF THE KASSENA-NANKANA DISTRICT MUTUAL HEALTH INSURANCE SCHEME"

BY

MENSAH CHARLES

(FAS/1200/06)

A PROJECT SUBMITTED TO THE UNIVERSITY FOR DEVELOPMENT STUDIES

FACULTY OF COMPUTATIONAL AND DEVELOPMENTAL MATHEMATICS,

IN PARTIAL FULFILLMENT OF THE REQUIREMENTS FOR THE AWARD OF Bsc. ACTUARIAL SCIENCE

JUNE, 2010

TABLE OF CONTENTS

DEDICATION

This research is dedicated to my parents: Mr. Francis Kingsley Mensah-Aborampah and Mrs. Philomena Buadoo. And final dedication goes to Mr. Samari David (Scheme Manager, Kassena-Nankana District Mutual Health Insurance Scheme) whose support and encouragement motivated me to this height.

ABSTRACT

The research reviewed the National Health Insurance Scheme and accessed the possibility of a single premium for decade. The whole research had its foundations from the specific objectives which were; to access the possibility of a single premium for a decade that is feasible enough to sustain the scheme, to identify alternative means of generating income to sustain the Kassena-Nankana District Mutual Health Scheme and to assess the perception of registered and potential clients on the NHIS. The research design employed was statistical survey and both qualitative and quantitative data were collected from a sample of fifty respondents. The research study has its justification from the current government's intention to implement a single premium system for the NHIS. The main hypothesis that "A single premium is feasible to improve healthcare in Ghana" was accepted with some few actuarial assumptions being made. The research findings emphasized the inclusion of age distribution as key variable to avoid all ages paying the same premium. Problem like moral hazards was addressed in this study and advocacy was suggested as a way of curbing it down. The administrative and accounting systems of NHIS must be fully computerized to help reduce the stress of working manually. Advocacy was also suggested as a solution to the problem of clients going for medications for non registered clients with their NHIS card.

Keywords; Insurance, Single premium, Health Inurance, Premium.

ACKNOWLEDGEMENT

I thank the Almighty God for providing me with the strength and knowledge to complete this course.

I am also indebted to a number of people who provided invaluable services in diverse ways towards the accomplishment of this task. Among them are: Mr. Yin Luu – Lecturer and Supervisor for the project for giving me a fatherly advice and guidance throughout the course of study.

I am also grateful to Mr. Solomon Sarpong – Acting Head Of Department (HOD) for being an inspirer, adviser and a mentor.

To Mr. Bankale Richard, I say many thanks for patiently being my guide and wonderful Lecturer for the four years of my academic study in the University.

I would also like to acknowledge my colleges and friends (Mr Ridwan Rufai.D and Mr. Mensah William,) for giving me their books for the research study. The Bolgatanga Municipal Library staff cannot be left out for their cooperation during the course of study.

CHAPTER ONE

1.0   Background

The National Health Insurance Scheme (NHIS) is an insurance policy enacted by government in the early years of 2000 to eradicate the "cash and carry" system and provide a better health care for all Ghanaians.(Ghanaweb.com-4th march 2010)

Historically, the health insurance in Ghana started as far back as 1992 when the first Community Health Insurance (CHI) scheme was started by the St. Theresa's Catholic Mission Hospital at Nkoranza. Agyepong Irene (2010). It proved popular and endured the test of time. In the mid 1990's, a unit was created in the Ministry of Health to establish the National Health Insurance (NHI) as an alternative to "cash and carry" health care delivery system in the country. The unit focused its efforts and resources on consultancies and feasibility studies for a pilot Social Health Insurance (SHI) scheme for the formal sector and organized groups such as cocoa farmers in the Eastern Region.Agyepong Irene (2010)

By 1999, the proposed SHI pilot collapsed without insuring anybody. Following the demise of the Eastern Region pilot, the Social Security and National Insurance Trust (SSNIT) started planning for another centralized health insurance scheme to be run by a company called Ghana Health Care Company. Like the Eastern Region pilot, it never took off despite some public expenditure on feasibility and software. Agyepong Irene (2010)

Following intense consultations with Ghana's international health development partners like World Health Organization (WHO), Danish International Development Agency (DANIDA) and International Labour Organization (ILO) and relevant national agencies and Non Governmental Organizations (NGO's), the Ghana NHIS was established with the *National Health Insurance Act* of 2003. The stated mission of the NHIS is "to ensure equitable universal access for all residents of Ghana to an acceptable quality of essential health services without out-of-pocket payment being required at the point of service use" (Ghana Ministry of Health, 2004a). The NHIS is regulated by the National Health Insurance Council (NHIC), headquartered in Accra. Regional and District offices of the

6

NHIC are being set up to decentralize the operations of the Scheme. The Council manages the National Health Insurance Fund (NHIF) through the collection, investment, disbursement, and administration of the Scheme. The Council also undertakes the licensing, regulation, and accreditation of healthcare providers. By the end of 2007, the NHIS had accredited 800 private healthcare providers in addition to government health facilities. Ghana Ministry of Health, (2008).The bill that was passed into National Insurance Act (NHIA) of 2003, required everybody resident in Ghana to be insured in the government sponsored district Mutual Health Organizations (MHO) financing of the NHIS was to be by individual premium payments and a 2.5% National Health Insurance Levy (NHIL).Agyepong Irene (2010). A National Health Insurance Council (NHIC) was to govern the NHIS. The objective of the council according to ACT 625 was "to ensure the implementation of a national health insurance policy that ensures access to basic healthcare services to all residents". Its responsibilities included registration, licensing and regulation of health insurance schemes and supervision of their operations. It was also responsible for granting accreditation to health care providers, monitoring their performance, and ensuring that healthcare services rendered to beneficiaries were of good quality. Agyepong Irene (2010). The current government stated in his manifesto for election 2008 that they were to going to find ways for Ghanaians to pay a single premium for a life time under the NHIS. NDC Manifesto (2008)

1.1 The history of the Kassena-Nankana District Mutual Health Insurance Scheme

The Kassena- Nankana District Mutual Health Insurance Scheme was started in 2003. Before the scheme kicked start, the District Task Force (DTF) and the District health team were tasked to start the sensitization of the NHIS in Kassena-Nankana.

In 2003, the legislative Instrument (LI) 1809 and ACT650 of the Health Insurance Act was passed by parliament.Officers were recruited for the NHISin September 2004 and the working staff took over from District Assembly in the same year.

The General Assembly (GA) then discussed on the formation of a constitution for the district health scheme on 23rd march 2005and appointment of the Board of Directors was

7

carried out in April 2005.On 1ˢᵗ November 2005, the scheme began its maiden operations and management of claims in Kassena-Nankana District. Preliminary Field Survey (2010)

1.2   Problem Statement

Several problems have been identified by the administrators and clients of the National Health Insurance Scheme undertaken by the Kassena-Nankana District. The problem of NHIS in the Kassena-Nankana district is divided into three (3) main parts namely administrative, clientele and service providers' problems.

ADMINISTRATIVE PROBLEMS

*Premium collection by installments; Even though it is stated in NHIS constitution that an adult can pay his or her premiums twelve(12) equal installments, the administrators complain of difficulty in managing the installment payments. Therefore clients are always advised and encouraged to pay their premiums in full or in two monthly equal payments. Adults who are not able to pay their premiums at once or by installments more than two are discouraged from joining the scheme because of its administrative difficulty. Field survey (2010)

*High Tariffs; Tariffs are also so high that the Kassena-Nankana Scheme owes the health providers huge amounts of money. Field survey (2010)

Tariffs are the monies paid for the bills submitted by health providers under the NHIS. Due to the constant leveled premium, that is GH₵ 8 paid by both the rich and the poor in the community and increase in the population, there is high level of indebtedness since lots of people in the scheme and are not paying the right premium they should pay for the scheme to be sustainable.

*Difficulty in verifying the authenticity of clients by health providers; Since the National Health Insurance Scheme is networked, that is between the District Mutual Health Administration and the Health providers, if a hospital/clinical is not hooked up or

8

linked by network, it makes it difficult to authenticate the validity of a member and to know if the member has renewed his membership or not.

*Inadequate Staff; There exist a problem of staff inadequacy at the Kassena-Nankana Mutual Health Centre and this makes them to rely on National Service personnel's. Also, qualifiedstaffs for the job are not enough. (Field survey, 2010)

*Politics ; Here, when there is a change of government, the management of scheme might be changed and this can negatively affect the effective running of the scheme because the new management might not continue with the effective strategies in place for the sustainability of the scheme in the district.

PROBLEMS FROM CLIENTS

*Expensive Premium; Upper East is rated one of the poorest regions in Ghana, and most of the inhabitants particularly the indigenes consider the current annual premium of GHC 8 to be expensive. Field Survey (2010).

*Some people also have the view that they do not usually fall sick so there is no reason for registering under the NHIS. They rather see it to be waste of financial resources. Field Survey (2010)

*Moral Hazards; These are the problems intentionally caused by clients who wants to take advantages of the liberal systems of NHIS. Several cases have been reported where a whole family intentionally visits the hospital when they are not sick but because they have been registered under NHIS.

*Abuse of the system; Someclients donot continue with their medications as prescribed by doctors thereby wasting the remaining drug received under the NHIS. War Memorial Hospital, Navrongo (2010)

PROBLEM FROM HEALTH PROVIDERS;

*Lack of quality health care; Due to the high patronage of the NHIS, the health facilities in the Kassena-Nankana district cannot match the number of registered clients thereby resulting in poor health care. The health providers are also not equipped very well resulting in deaths of registered clients.

*Inadequate drug provision; Hospitals are not also able to provide all the needed drugs for the registered patients and this results in they asking the patient to buy the unavailable drugs at the pharmacy and drug stores.Field Survey(2010)

1.3 General objectives

This study is aimed at finding out how the NHIS is performing in Kassena-Nankana District and the feasibility of a single premium for a decade.

SPECIFIC OBJECTIVES

1. To access thepossibilityof a possible single premium for a decade that is feasible enough to sustain the scheme.
2. To identify alternatives means of generating income to sustain the Kassena-Nankana District Mutual Health Scheme.
3. To asses the perception of registered and potential clients under the NHIS.

1.4 Justification

The NHIS plays an important role in providing accessible health care to Ghanaians and sought to eradicate the then concept of "cash and carry" in the health care delivery system. The government authorized a mandatory2.5% levy to be deducted from SSNITcontributors to augment regular premium that clients pay under the scheme. The study seeks to explore the prospects of the current government intension to implement a single premium system by assessing the viability and/or feasibility of a single premium that is sufficient to sustain the health insurance system for at least a decade.

1.5   Hypothesis

Ho; Asingle premium for a decade is feasible to improve health care in Ghana

H1;A single premium for a decade is not feasible to improve health care in Ghana.

1.6   Scope and expected outcome

This research will be carried out within the Kassena- Nankana District in the Upper East Region of Ghana. The research will involve fifty (50) inhabitants of Navrongo.

It is expected that at the end of the project, tangible and effective solutions to the administrative problems, client problems and health provider problems would be obtained.

The sustainability and viability of a single premium for a decade would be known and it's projections given.

This project would also identify various ways by which the District can generate some funding to help support the scheme.

CHAPTER TWO

LITERATURE REVIEW

2.0   INTRODUCTION

Health insurance is a type of insurance designed to pay the costs associated with health care. Health Insurance plan pays the bills from physicians, hospitals and other providers of medical services. By doing so, health insurance protects people from financial hardship caused by large or unexpected medical bills. (Microsoft Encarta-2009). Because of unexpected financial losses that come our way everyday, it is very prudent to join health insurance scheme to indemnify you when you fall sick. Individuals obtain their health insurance from private organizations or from government. In Ghana, the National Health Insurance Scheme (NHIS) is an insurance policy enacted by government in 2003 to eradicate the "cash and carry " health care delivery system established in 1985 (LI 1313) and provide a better health care for all Ghanaians. Agyepong et al (2007)

Premiums are payment an individual policyholder makes in exchange for the promise of financial assistance for the loss occurred. (Microsoft Encarta-2009). Premiums paid for health insurance schemes are to indemnify one from his or her financial loss caused by medical cost of sickness. Single premiumlife insurance is a type of life insurance where you pay a lump sum on a life insurance policy that stays valid until you die. Single premium life insurance plan offers a wide range of investments and withdrawal options. (Babyboomercaretaker.com-2007). The single premium life policy builds' up cash quickly because the entire policy is paid in full. Just like any other life insurance policy, the benefit depends upon the amount of money you pay, your health and your age. Since single premiums life policy are usually long term, it gives ample time for the invested premium to mature. The theoretical review, which forms the basis of this chapter, is structured as follows:

   *Insurance

   *Premiums

   -single premiums

   -critiques of the NHIS

*Means of generating income to sustain a scheme

*Chapter summary

2.1   Insurance

The New Encyclopedia Britannica 2007 identifies insurance as a method of coping with risk. Its primary function is to substitute certainty for uncertainty as regards the economic cost of loss-producing events. Insurance may be defined more formally as a system under which the insurer, for a consideration usually agreed upon in advance promises to reimburse the insured or to render services to the insured in the event that certain accidental occurrence result in losses during a given period.

The 15th Edition of the New Encyclopedia Britannica continues to explain health insurance as a system for the advance financing of medical expenses by means of contributions or taxes paid into a common fund to pay all or part of health services specified in an insurance policy or law. It goes on to further identity the key elements in health insurance as payments of premiums, pooling of funds and eligibility for benefits on the basis of contribution.

2.2   Critiques of the NHIS

Malaka Grant of the Ghana Health Service wrote an article about the proleriat sign up of the scheme, that is there has been little literature about the scheme but this research into the scheme indicates that most people are aware of the scheme but they are not joining because of the long waiting period for; the NHIS identity card and the high premiums charged.

He also continues in his article by saying NHIS does not cover most surgeries which is another reason why people are not joining. Ghana Health Service, (2008)

2.3   MEANS OF GENERATING INCOME TO SUSTAIN A SCHEME

*Taxation has been identified as one of the effective ways of generating income for the government. The most important reason for this is that the function of taxes is not simply to raise revenue but to reduce private demand so that resources can be released for public

sector use. Aulid D.A.L. et al(1982). Now narrowing it down to the Kassena-Nankana district, the district can generate income to sustain the scheme by increasing taxes within the community. Taxes paid when dumping rubbish in the community, taxes paid by petty traders, property rate for Kassena-Nankana and taxes paid for land valuationcould be increased percentage wise to help subsidize the scheme. Land valuation taxes have been included because the government pays some percentage to the chiefs of the area from where the money was generated for development.

*Kassena-Nanka District could also generate funds from the festival celebrated in the district.There are many possible revenue streams when organizing a festival. If properly managed, you should make a handsome profit. GoudieEric, (2010)

2.4   Chapter summary

This chapter brought to light, literature and articles that have been published about the study. It also followed the chronological order outlined in the introduction and dissected the sub-heading with various definitions. It also explained insurance as a system under which the insurer, for a consideration usually agreed upon in advance promises to reimburse the insured or to render services to the insured in the event that certain accidental occurrence result in losses during a given period. It also gave literature about a critique of NHIS (Malaka Grant) and also suggested ways of generating income for the scheme.

CHAPTER THREE

3.0 RESEARCH METHODOLOGIES

In the previous chapters, it introduced and provided literature to support the study. This chapter however will dive deep into the methods and techniques that were adopted to collect the data for the analysis of the study in chapter four. The research design and methodology of the study have been described under the following sub-headings:

The research design;

The population of the study;

The sample of the study;

The data collection technique;

Chapter summary;

These are the chronological steps taken for the chapter to be completed

3.1 The research design

This study in a long run serves two separate purposes that is reviewing the NHIS and coming out with a single premium that may be feasible under the NHIS for a decade. Using statistical survey as the research design, qualitative and quantitative data would be employed in my research design. This research design avails it self as a mixed method under the multiple method choice (curran and Blackburn, 2001: Tashakkori and Teddlie, 2003).

3.2 Qualitative data technique

It involves using data whose measurements scales are inherently categorical. Information gathered from the self administered survey will be analyzed using pie chart to know how clients are rating the health insurance schemes that is "very good, good, bad, worse"

3.3 Quantitative data technique

It involved data that are numeric and which define value or quantity. This method will be used to obtain data on the amount of premium to pay under the single premium for a decade.

A mathematical model will be created based on variables like the number of registered clients, amounts contributed to the fund and the Insurance liability, to get the rate at which losses occur. DeMoivre law and other models like the continues model will be used for the premium calculation model.

The short fall of this fund will be catered for by accessing other sources to generating income in order to support the scheme. One way is by creating a pooling fund for prominent indigenes of Kassena-Nankana who stays in the district and indigenes else around the globe. When these regular contributions are paid willingly, it will help to support the Kassena-Nankana District Mutual Health Scheme

3.4 The population of the study

The study population covers the entire Kassena-Nankana District which can be found in the Upper East Region of Ghana. The region has a total population of about 963000 with only 367000 registered under the scheme. (The NHIS, National Headquarters, August 2007). It is estimated that about 38.1% are registered under the scheme as at June 2007. The sample of the study was therefore selected from this population.

3.5 The Sample Size of the Study

The study sample was selected entirely from the inhabitants in the Kassena-Nankana District. A sample size of fifty (50) respondents was chosen from occupations like teaching, dressmaking, petty trading and students. The method of selection was made basically on random sampling to prevent biasness.

3.6   Data collection techniques

Using quantitative and qualitative data for analysis demanded that separate techniques be applied. For the quantitative data, secondary data was collected from the Kassena-Nankana District Mutual Health Insurance scheme. Schedules and well structured questionnaires were used to gather information about the qualitative data. A day was used to collect the quantitative data whiles another day was used to collect qualitative data.

3.7   Chapter summary

Chapter three explained stages that were employed to collect the field data for the analysis to be done in chapter four. The qualitative and quantitative data techniques were used to satisfy the non numerical and numerical values that would be obtained from the research. Due to financial constraint, the sample size was limited to fifty (50) respondents and all respondents were selection at random. A combination of observation, interviews for taking field notes and well structured questionnaires was employed to collect the field data for the study.

CHAPTER FOUR

4.0   RESEARCH FINDINGS, ANALYSIS AND DISCURSIONS

The previous chapters of this study talked about the contextual, theoretical and the descriptive aspects of the study, whichare methodologies that will be used to collect the needed data. This chapter focuses on the analysis from the field and the secondary data given. The qualitative data collected under the survey was coded for the analysis. Microsoft Excel spreadsheet was used to analyze the qualitative data. Quantitative data was also addressed in relation to the objectives of the study and the hypothesis of the study.

The findings, analyses and discussion of the field and secondary data have been presented in the following chronological order;

4.1 Background of the respondents

4.2 Membership profile

4.3 Designing a model for the single premium calculation

4.4 The sufficiency of the premium to provide for the claim.

4.5 The probability that the net single premium will cover the benefit (feasibility)

4.6 Chapter summary

4.1   Background of the respondents

This part of the chapter throws light on the personal profile of the forty five (45) respondents that is their age groups, and gender. The forty five respondents for the qualitative elements of the study consisted of 56% males and 44% females. 68.9% of the respondents were aged from 18 to 59, 20% of the respondents went for ages from 60 and above whiles 11.1% of the population were within the ages 0 to 17.

4.2   Membership profile

The membership profile section of this chapter describes with charts the number of males and females in the National health scheme in Kassena-Nankana District, number of males and females not in the scheme, the educational of those who did not join the scheme, the

quality of health care registered clients get at the health center, the availability of drugs covered under the scheme and the perception of registered client about the scheme.

Figure 4.1

NUMBER OF MALES AND FEMALES IN THE NHIS

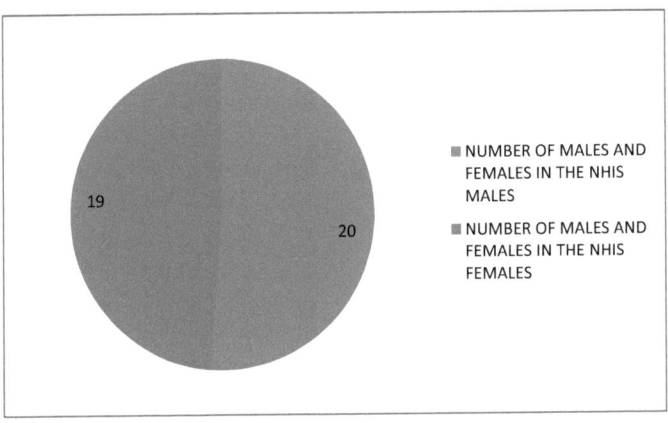

Field survey (2010)

From the pie chart above, we can see that out of 45 respondents, 39 are registered under the scheme and aremade up of 20 males and 19 females registered under the scheme. The closeness of the populations indicates that both genders are interested in the scheme.

Figure 4.2

NUMBER OF MALES AND FEMALES NOT IN THE
SCHEME

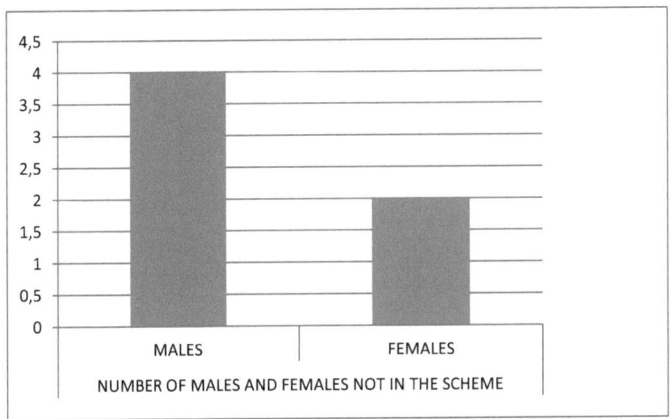

Field survey (2010)

This bar chart also draws a clear picture of males not joining the scheme. Out of the 6 respondents who did not join the scheme, 4 were males and 2 were females.

Figure 4.3

THE EDUCATIONAL LEVEL OF THOSE WHO DID NOT JOIN THE
SCHEME

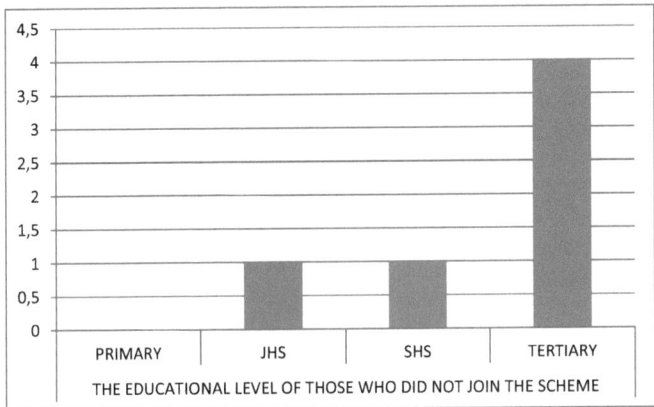

Field Survey (2010)

This chart clearly shows that the well educated in the community are not really buying
into the scheme.

Figure 4.4

QUALITY HEALTH CARE WITH THE NHIS CARD AT THE
HEALTH SCHEME

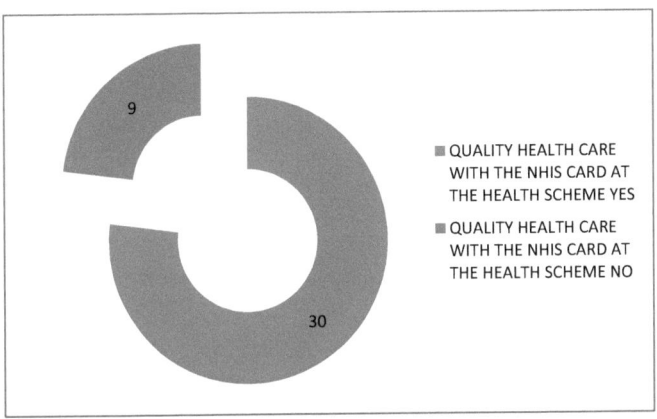

QUALITY HEALTH CARE WITH THE NHIS CARD AT THE HEALTH SCHEME YES

QUALITY HEALTH CARE WITH THE NHIS CARD AT THE HEALTH SCHEME NO

Field Survey (2010)

The doughnut chart clearly indicates that about 77% of the respondents appreciate the quality health care given them when they visit the health center with their NHIS card whiles only 23% are not satisfied with the quality of the services they received.

Figure 4.5

AVAILABILITY OF ALL DRUGS COVERED UNDER THE
NHIS

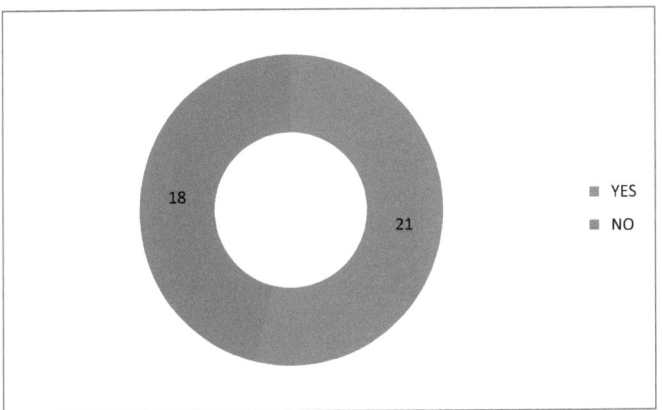

Field Survey (2010)

The doughnut chart above throws more light on the drug delivery system administered by
health centers under the scheme. Out of the 39 registered respondents, 21 said they get all
their drugs that have been covered under NHIS from the health centers whiles 18
responded negativeto this statement.

Figure 4.6

PERCEPTION OF REGISTERED CLIENTS ABOUT THE SCHEME

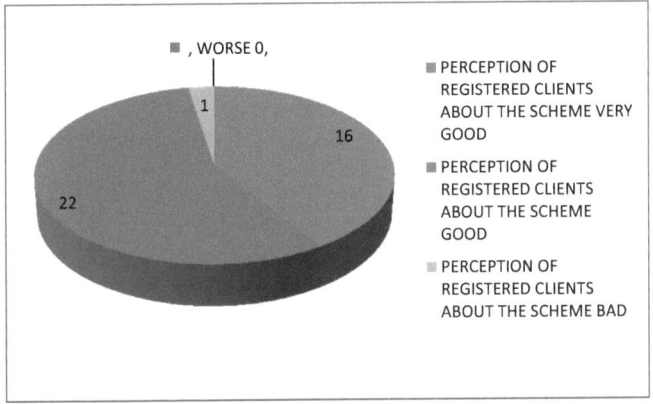

Field Survey (2010)

This is the final analysis that fulfills the third specific objective of the study which is the people's perception about the NHIS and from the pie chart; it clearly tells that the clients are really commending the Scheme for their effort. More than half of the respondent said it was good, whiles quite a number of them also said it was very good and only 1 respondent said the scheme was bad. Generally the people of Kassena-Nankana have accepted and praised the good work of the scheme.

4.3   Designing a model for the single premium calculation

A basic single premium for health insurance to a person aged (X) provides full access to health care for a decade and ends when the 10years is over, or the insured dies, or the insured withdraws from the scheme.

In the **continues model,** the assumption is that thebenefit ends immediately when one withdraws from the scheme, dies or ends the insurance cover period.

24

Continuous case

Let GH₵1.00 be the average cost of paying a client's bill by the scheme in Kassena-Nankana for 10 years from issue. Since death or withdrawal occurs at random future life times, the claim has a random present value ($\bar{Z}x$)

$\bar{Z}x = e^{-\delta T}$

Where δ= force of interest (bank interest rate)

      T= random future life time

      e= natural log

The expected value of $\bar{Z}x$ is denoted by $\bar{A}x$ and is called the **Net Single Premium** for a decade or the **Actuarial Present Value** of the claim. Since $\bar{Z}x$ is a function of random future life time T, the actuarial present value;

$\bar{A}x = E[\bar{Z}x] = E[e^{\delta T}] = \int_{t=0}^{\omega-x} e^{-\delta T} f(T)\, dt$

Where $\bar{A}x$=Net Single Premium for a decade.

ω= the maximum age the insured will get to before his or her insurance period ends.

f(T)= function of future life time (T)

dt = Derivative of random future life time

$\bar{A}x = \int_{t=0}^{\omega-x} e^{-\delta T} tP_x\mu_{x+t}\, dt$

where $tP_x\mu_{x+t}$ =A person aged (X) lives t more years and ends his insurance period at x+t

Here t=10 years

Assuming the person's age (x)=18 years,

With deMoivre's law, where

$T\sim\mu(0,\omega-x)$= this means that the insured can enjoy the scheme for the maximum insured policy period, that is 10years. Because if x= 18 and ω is the maximum age the insured can attain in the scheme and that is 28 years.

Now $tP_x\mu_{x+t} = f(T) = 1/(\omega-x)$

=1/ (28-18)

          =1/10

We recall that $\bar{A}x = \int_{t=0}^{\omega-x} e^{-\delta T} tP_x\mu_{x+t} dt$

But $tP_x\mu_{x+t}$=1/10

$\bar{A}x = \int_0^{10} e^{-\delta(T)} 1/10\, dt$

$\bar{A}x = 1/10 \int_0^{10} e^{-\delta(T)} \, dt$

$\bar{A}x = 1/10[-e^{-\delta\,(T)}/\delta, 0, 10]$

$\bar{A}x = 1/10[(-e^{-\delta(10)}/\delta) + (e^{\delta(0)}/\delta)]$

$\bar{A}x = 1/10[(1-e^{-\delta(10)})/\delta]$

Assuming the force of interest which is the current banking interest rate is 25%

$\bar{A}x = 1/10[(1-e^{-0.25(10)})/0.25]$

$\bar{A}x = 0.3671660006$

$\bar{A}x \approx 0.4$

This means that GHC0.4 will be paid as a single premium to cover the health insurance for a decade.

4.4 The sufficiency of the net single premium to provide for the claim

Considering a premium of GH 40p paid at issue, it grows with interest at future life time T to $e^{\delta T}$. $\bar{A}x$. The premium is **sufficient** to provide for the claim if;

$e^{\delta T}$. $\bar{A}x > 1$ or $\bar{A}x > e^{-\delta T}$

therefore,

$e^{\delta T}$. $\bar{A}x = e^{(0.25*10)}*0.4 = 4.872997584$ and this is greater than 1.

Also,

$\bar{A}x = 0.4$ and this is greater than $e^{-\delta T}$ which is 0.0821, therefore it can be concluded that the premium is **sufficient**.

4.5 The probability that the net single premium will cover the claim (feasibility)

Computing the probability that the net single premium will cover the claim (feasibility)

$\ln \bar{A}x/-\delta = \ln 0.3671166/-0.25$

$\qquad = 4.007764868$

Therefore the probability that the net single premium will cover the claim over the decade

is $= \int_{4.007}^{10} (\frac{1}{10}) \, dt$

$= [t/10, 10, 4.007]$

$= 1-0.4007$

=0.5993

≈0.6

This means that the Net Single Premium will cover the claim with a probability of **0.6** and therefore making it feasible.

4.6   Chapter summary

This chapter clears the air about the research findings, analysis and discussions that were undertaken in this study. Charts like the bar and pie charts were used to analyze and know the perception about NHIS using the forty five respondents for the study. Using the continues case, a model has been deduced and it's sufficiency and feasibility was calculated assuming GH₵1.00 as the average cost of catering for a registered client for 10 years. Using this same assumption, it was deduced that if a client should pay GH 40p, it could sustain for 10 years with interest rate at 25%. However, this model should always be adjusted to fit one's locality and age that is a 40 year old man should not pay the same premium as an 18 year old person. This should be so because you grow old you become prone to diseases.

CHAPTER FIVE

THE RESEARCH SUMMARY, RECOMMENDATIONS AND CONCLUSIONS

5.0   Introduction

The National Health Insurance Scheme is a very important tool for Ghana's development and should be held with high esteem. It seeks to provide quality health care delivery for all residents of Ghana. A review of this scheme came out with some challenges and some potentials and this chapter will come out with findings, recommendation and conclusions. In the Kassena-Nankana district, the registered clients are enjoying the scheme but there are problems that need to be addressed in the shortest possible time.

5.1   Summary of findings

This is a summary of all the findings in this research survey

5.1.1   Problems and possible solutions

- ADMINISTRATIVE PROBLEMS

- Premium collection by installment;Administrators complain of difficulty in managing premium paid in twelve equal installment even though the NHIS constitution allows it. Therefore clients are always advised and encouraged to pay their premiums in full or in two monthly equal payments. Adults who are not able to pay their premiums at once or by installments more than two are discouraged from joining the scheme because of it's administrative difficulty.

- This problem can be effectively addressed when Kassena-Nankana district mutual health insurance scheme employ qualified staff for the scheme. Since most of its workers are national service personnels, they do not get adequate training and experience because of the perception that they might leave the institution at the end of the service period. Now dissecting deep into this problem, the scheme's administrative and accounting systems must be fully computerized. Continues registration occurring in the system becomes tedious when every thing is done on paper that is why the workers can not keep recording twelve equal installments of a particular client. But when a

CHAPTER TEN

THE RESEARCH SUMMARY, RECOMMENDATIONS AND CONCLUSIONS

computerized system is created and every body has a separate account, retrieving the files from the computer is far easier than the one done manually.

- Politics; Changing government might cause a change in the management of the scheme and this might slow down the scheme's progress.

- Changing management with respect to change of government retards the progress of the institution since every management has it's own agenda. If this institution is made autonomous on without any political influence, there might be much progress

- PROBLEM FROM CLIENTS

- Moral Hazards; Some registered clients intentionally visit the hospital whiles they are not sick just because they have the NHIS card.

- Advocacy on behalf of the scheme operators and the health providers can help curve down this problem. Organized forums in the district about moral hazard might help reduce it.

- Abuse of the system;Clients go to the hospital pretending they are sick just to receive the drugs for an unregistered client.

- Advocacy can also be used to address the problem effectively. Educating the public through their local radio stations and organized forums on the serious health implications this may cause will help refrain people from the practice.

- PROBLEM FROM HEALTH PROVIDERS

- Inadequate drug provision; Hospitals are not also able to provide all the needed drugs for the registered patients and this results in they asking the patient to buy the unavailable drugs at the pharmacy and drug stores.

- The Scheme should do its possible best to provide hospitals with the needed covered drugs especially with those in the rural communities.

5.1.2   Means of generating income to sustain the scheme

- Taxation is one effective way of generating income to sustain the scheme. Taxes derived from dumping rubbish could be increased to help support the scheme. Also taxes paid by petty traders in Kassena-Nankana district could be increased by 20%   to help generate income to sustain the health scheme. This has got its justification from the environmental pollution these petty traders cause by selling.

- Kassena-Nankana district could also get some funding from a well organized festival. Festival bring a lot of foreigners to the community, therefore if well organized, it might help create a fund to sustain the scheme.
- A special fund can be created for the residents and well wishers of Kassena-Nankana where they can make contributions at their own will to help sustain the scheme.

5.1.3 POSSIBILITY OF A SINGLE PREMIUM

- In chapter four, a model was created for a single premium for a decade from serveral models like deMoivres Law and Force of constant mortality. Since secondary data could not be found on the tariffs paid according to the age intervals , some assumptions to distinguish premium. Clients above forty(40) should not pay the same premium as clients below twenty-five(25) since people above forties have more health complications than twenty-five year old. The model was proved to be feasible when its probability to cover the scheme was more than 0.5 . The net single premium for a decade was found to GHȻ 0.4 assuming GHȻ 1.00 is the average cost of bill the scheme pays on a registered client for a decade.

5.2 Recommendations

Considering the critical role that health plays in the nation's development, it is recommended that; further studies be carried out on the possibility of a single premium, further research carried out on alternative means of generating income to sustain the NHIS, and further research be carried out on the perception of registered and potential clients under the NHIS on a large scale

5.2.1 POSSIBILITY OF A SINGLE PREMIUM

- The researcher recommends that if Government wants to come out with a single premium for a life time, then age interval distribution should be seriously considered. Also it is recommended that NHIS management should start taking data on the tariffs paid by the scheme for every age from age 18 to age 60 to aid actuaries come out with a correct single premium.

5.2.2 MEANS OF GENERATING INCOME TO SUSTAIN THE SCHEME

- It is recommended that government should take a critical look at other sources of funding apart from the taxes we pay if it wants to go with the single premium. The Scheme should also go into long term investments to enable the fund sustain the scheme.

5.2.3 PERCEPTION OF REGISTERED AND POTENTIAL CLIENTS UNDER THE SCHEME

- Since this research had a small sample size (50), it is recommended that a larger survey be taken to cover the entire nation to know how people are really rating the scheme and what they think the scheme lacks.

5.3 Chapter Summary

This chapter discusses the findings of the research and comes out with recommendations that will sustain the scheme. Its starts with an introduction to the chapter. Under the summary of findings, problems and possible solutions were given to the outcome of the findings. Recommendations were also given to the respective stakeholders of the Scheme and this was treated in relation to the specific objectives of the study. With the first specific objective that is the possibility of a single premium, it was recommended by the researcher that if government wants to come out with a single premium, then age interval distribution should be considered. It was also recommended that government should take another look at other sources of funding apart from the taxes so that the single premium could be achieved and this fulfilled the second specific objective. With the third objective, it was recommended that a larger survey be taken to cover the entire nation to know the perception people have about the NHIS.

REFRENCES

Agyepong Irene(2010),Historic context of NHIS, Daily Graphic, February 24th 2010-Accra

Agyepong.I.,Oppong.J.(2007);Ghana HealthServices and Abt Association, Inc2007;WB2007

Atta Mills(His Excellency Presedent Of the Republic of Ghana)(2008), *NDC manifesto 2008*

Goudie Eric (2010), Ways of generating Income from Festivals, *Helium Inc*-America

Microsoft Encarta (2009), Definition of Health Insurance

Malaka Grant(2008*), CBS news report-Ghana Health Service* –Accra

OppongR.Joseph,Mensah Joseph and Schmidt M.Christoph(2004a), Ghana Ministry of Health

OppongR.Joseph,Mensah Joseph and Schmidt M.Christoph(2008), Ghana Ministry of Health

OppongR.Joseph,Mensah Joseph and Schmidt M.Christoph, *Ghana's National Health Insurance Scheme in the context of the Health MDGs- An Empirical Evaluation using propensity score matching*

OwusuAdobea (2009), PRO-MHI Conference Lilongwe, Malawi-2nd and 3rd Dec 2009-Accra

Rice, Thomas, and Kathleen Morrison. "Patient Cost-sharing for Medical Services: A Review of the Literature and Implications for Health Care Reform." *Medical Care Review*, Vol. 51(3): 235-287, March 1994.

Rice, Thomas and Kenneth Thorpe. "Income-related Costing Sharing in Health Insurance." *Health Affairs*, Vol. 12(1): 21- 39, Spring 1993.

The New Encyclopedia Britannica 2007, Insurance

The New Encyclopedia Britannica 2007-15th edition, Health Insurance

The NHIS Constitution(2003*),* National Headquarters-Accra

SITE REFERENCES

(http//www.ghanaweb.com),accessed 2010 March 4

(http//www.Babyboomercaretaker.com) accessed 2007

(http//www.ghanaweb.com),Berkoh Francis, accessed 2010 April 4

APPENDIX

QUESTIONNAIRE

"A REVIEW OF THE NATIONAL HEALTH INSURANCE SCHEME AND THE POSSIBILITY OF A SINGLE PREMIUM FOR A DECADE". Ref ☐ ☐

A case study of the Kassena-Nankana District Mutual Health Insurance Scheme.

The researcher is a final year student of the University for Development Studies working on the above topic. Any information given is for academic use only. Your responses will be kept confidential.

Please tick where appropriate.

SECTION A (**Respondent's personal profile**)

1. Age ☐ up to 18 years

   ☐ 19years to 59 years

   ☐ 60years and above

2. Gender ☐ Male ☐ Female

3. Occupation ☐ teaching /lecturing ☐ dress making

   ☐ Petty trading ☐ student

Other (Specify)……………………

4. Qualification (level of education)

☐ Primary   ☐ J.H.S

☐ S.H.S   ☐ Tertiary

5. Religion

Christianity ☐   Islam ☐   Traditional ☐

SECTION B (Membership Profile)

6. Are you under any health scheme?   ☐ Yes, please specify…………………………………..

       ☐ No

7. Have you joined the National Health Insurance Scheme (N.H.I.S)?

       ☐ Yes   ☐ No

8. If no, do you have intensions of joining the N.H.I.S?

       ☐ Yes   ☐ No

9. If no, what is stopping you from joining?

☐ Finance   ☐ Religion   ☐ duration for NHIS card

Other (Specify)……………………………………………………………

34

10. If you are an N.H.I.S member, are you enjoying the scheme?

☐ Yes   ☐ No

11. If no, please your reason

....

....

12. Do you get quality health care with your NHIS card in the health centers?

☐ Yes   ☐ No

13. Do you get all your drugs that have been covered under the NHIS?

☐ Yes   ☐ No

14. What do you think about the attention you get at the hospital with the NHIS card?

☐ Very good   ☐ Good

☐ Bad   ☐ Worse

15. Would you like to renew your health insurance if your insurance period ends?

☐ Yes   ☐ No

16. If no, please give your reason

....

....

....

17. How would you describe the scheme?

☐ Very good   ☐ Good

☐ Bad   ☐ Worse

THANKYOU FOR YOUR COOPERATION!!!!!